WAS SHAKESPEARE REALLY SHAKESPEARE?

PETER LACEY

Alphabet Publishing

www.AlphabetPublish.com

Is the most famous author in English actually a fake? Some historians and literary scholars wonder whether William Shakespeare actually wrote the plays and poetry that are attributed to him. They believe there may have been a conspiracy to hide the true author of *Romeo and Juliet*, *Macbeth*, and all his other famous plays. But what is their evidence, and who was the real Shakespeare?

INTRODUCTION

William Shakespeare is one of the best known authors of all time. He was born in England in 1564, wrote a lot of plays and poetry, and then died in 1616. But after his death, his writing has continued to be read and performed and celebrated. Even today, people continue to make new movies from his work. If you have ever heard of the love story *Romeo and Juliet*, then you already know something about Shakespeare.

Though many people do know something about Shakespeare, nobody knows everything. He lived more than 400 years ago, and many details of his life have been lost or were never recorded, including his birthday—we *think* it's in April, but nobody recorded the exact day. As people have tried to better understand the famous author, the evidence they can and cannot find has led some to question whether the man named William Shakespeare was really the person who wrote the famous plays.

Several conspiracy theories about Shakespeare's identity exist. One theory is that many different people, a team of both men and women, actually wrote his plays and used the name Shakespeare as a pseudonym. Other theories claim a different famous man such as the Earl of Oxford or Sir Francis Bacon secretly wrote as Shakespeare. The most dramatic theory claims Shakespeare was actually an author named Christopher Marlowe who got in trouble with the government and faked his death.

Do any of these theories have strong evidence? Did Shakespeare really exist? And will the truth about his identity always be a mystery?

Introductory Questions

1. What do you already know about Shakespeare?

2. Have you seen any of his plays (or a movie based on one of his plays) or read any of his poetry?

3. Do you have a favorite?

4. Why might someone write under a pseudonym?

5. Who is your favorite author?

6. What have you read by them and why do you like them?

CONTENTS

THE PERSON

We know the basic facts about William Shakespeare's early life, but not much more. He was born in England in 1564, probably in April. His small hometown is called Stratford-upon-Avon and is over 90 miles away from London—a distance that would have seemed even farther in the time before modern transportation.

Believed to be William Shakespeare, attributed to John Taylor.

Shakespeare got married when he was 18 years old. His wife, Anne Hathaway, was 26 at the time. They had three children, a daughter born in 1583 and a twin boy and girl, born in 1585.

Believed to be Anne Hathaway, by Nathaniel Curzon

Eventually, Shakespeare moved to London where he became famous and successful. The move probably happened around 1585, when he was in his early 20s. It makes sense he would move to the capital of England to look for success, but like many aspects of his early life, we don't know exactly when or have any evidence why he chose to move.

The time between his marriage in Stratford and the first record of his work in London

Shakespeare's birthplace

is sometimes referred to as his "lost years" because we know almost nothing about it. His name is mentioned twice in legal documents. There was a case regarding family property. William Shakespeare may have appeared in court in London in 1588 as well.

Anne Hathaway's family home

Biographers have reported many different stories. Some say he was a schoolmaster or a law clerk. Others say his first job in the theatre in London was taking care of horses. It was even rumored that he ran to London to avoid being arrested for hunting animals on land belonging to a noble, Sir Thomas Lucy. There is no strong evidence for any of these stories, though. What we do know for sure

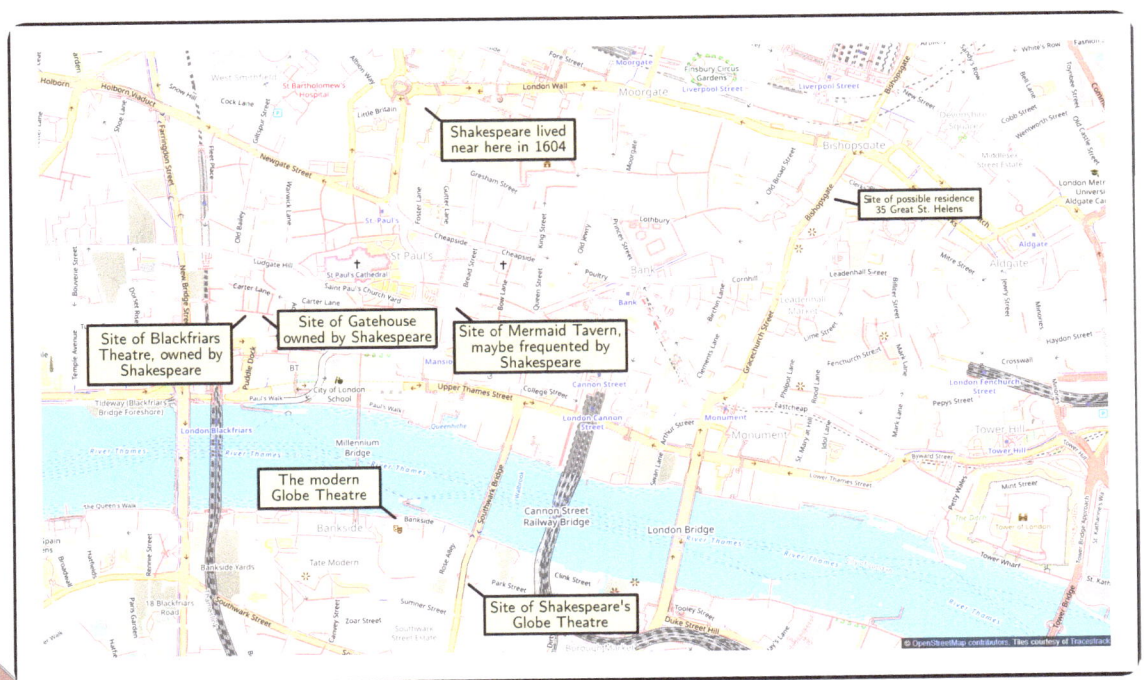

PLAYS, PLAYWRIGHTS, AND STAGES

Shakespeare lived hundreds of years before technology for movies and television was invented, but that doesn't mean people didn't watch stories acted out by famous actors. People in those days got together at theaters to watch dramas, romances, and comedies acted out in-person on a stage.

A story that's meant to be acted out on a stage is called a play, and the author who writes a play is a playwright. Shakespeare didn't only write plays, but many people think of him as a playwright because his most famous work was written to be acted on a stage.

One of the most well-known stages in London was the place that was built for Shakespeare's plays. It was called The Globe Theatre and was the place where his most famous plays were first seen hundreds of years ago. Though the original building was destroyed a long time ago, you can visit a reconstruction of the building in London and experience what it was like to watch a story acted in this style during Shakespeare's life.

People still write and perform plays today, and many people enjoy going to see actors perform in-person on stages. New and old plays are performed in famous places like Broadway in New York City, and there is a good chance you can watch a play on stage somewhere in your city.

is that his success writing plays and poetry began in the 1590s and lasted until he retired in 1613.

During his career in London, Shakespeare was a member of a group of actors called Lord Chamberlain's Men. Not only did he write plays for the group, but he was a part-owner of the company and also one of the actors who performed on stage. He seems to have been a truly talented and busy man.

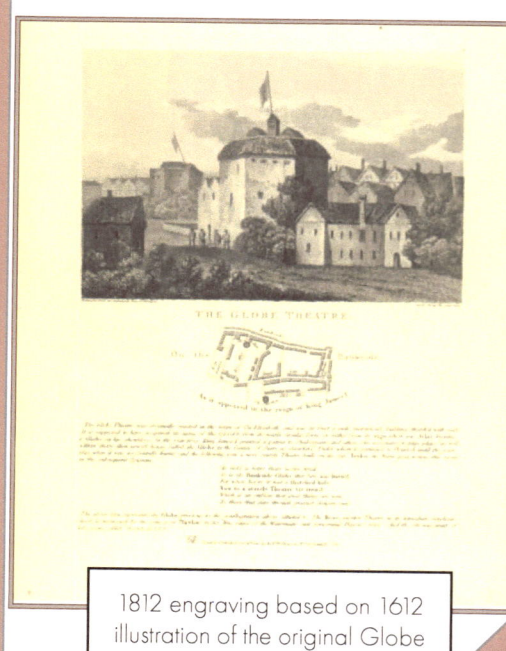

1812 engraving based on 1612 illustration of the original Globe

In 1599, Lord Chamberlain's Men finished building a new theater for their plays. They named it The Globe Theatre, and many of Shakespeare's famous works were first performed there.

Modern reconstruction of The Globe

At The Globe, his acting company was so successful that they won the patronage of King James I and changed their name to The King's Men. Needless to say, by that time, Shakespeare was considered one of the best playwrights in London. In addition to his theatrical work, he had also become very wealthy through real estate investments and had already bought one of the most expensive houses in Stratford in 1597. No doubt, his professional fame and business accomplishments seem to be at odds with what we know about his humble, rural background.

After retiring in 1613, Shakespeare died in his hometown, Stratford, in 1616. Like most other parts of his personal life, we have no details and can only wonder how and why. He had written his will a month before, and wrote that was in "perfect health" at the time. One story goes that he drank too

Interior of reconstruction of The Globe

SHAKESPEARE'S FAMOUS QUOTES

Shakespeare wrote 38 plays that we know of, including comedies, tragedies, and histories. Some are incredibly famous, and the words of his most famous plays have been quoted over and over through the years. Have you ever heard of these plays and their famous quotes?

Hamlet — A tragedy about a prince who discovers his uncle has murdered his father, married his mother, and taken over the kingdom. How will Prince Hamlet get his revenge?

"To be, or not to be, that is the question"
"This above all: To thine own self be true."

Macbeth — Macbeth is a noble who is told by witches that he will become king of Scotland. Macbeth eventually kills the king, but this starts a war that ends with tragedy.

"Out, out brief candle! Life's but a walking shadow, a poor player, That struts and frets his hour upon the stage, And then is heard no more"

much and fell ill, but experts dismiss this explanation as only a rumor. After his death, his work has continued to be read and performed and celebrated up to the present day.

THE MYSTERY

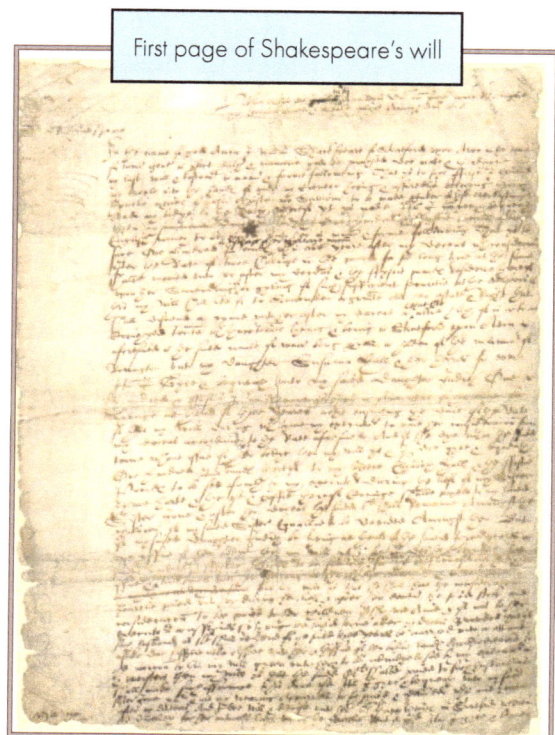

First page of Shakespeare's will

Not much is known about Shakespeare's childhood or personal life, and what we do know suggests he had a rather ordinary life. Because of this, some scholars believe he did not have the background to become such a prolific and highly successful writer. They believe that someone who became the most famous author in the English language would have gone to the best schools and lived an upper class lifestyle, having access to high society. But this is not true for Shakespeare. Even though many of his plays are about royal life and high society, his hometown of Stratford was in the countryside far from London.

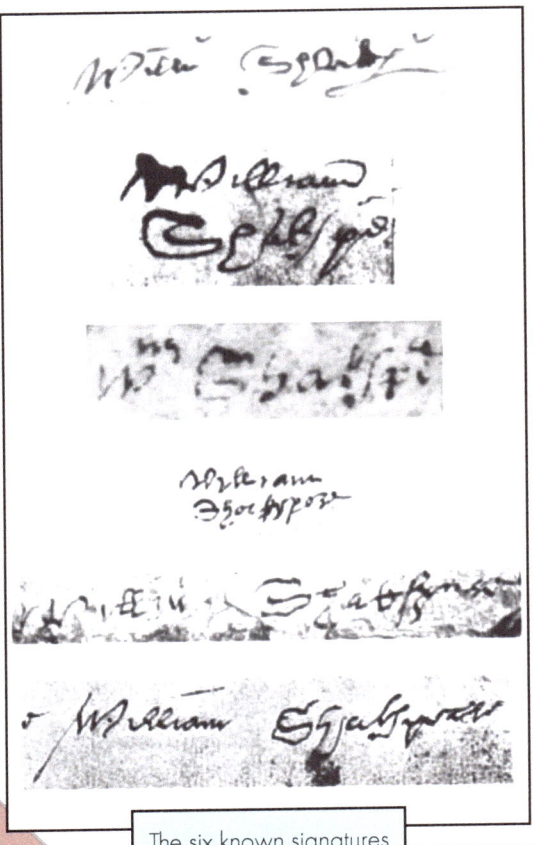

The six known signatures of Shakespeare

As You Like It — A romantic comedy about a woman who disguises herself as a man in order to get close to the man she loves.

> "All the world's a stage,
> and all the men and
> women merely players."

The Tempest — A Duke loses his power to his brother. He tries to use his magical powers to get revenge, but his spirit helper Ariel has other plans.

> "We are such stuff as dreams are made on"

King Richard III — Based on the history of a real king of England, Richard III imprisons his brother and kills his nephews to try to take over the throne.

> "Now is the winter of our discontent"

Romeo and Juliet — Teenagers from two feuding families fall in love. Friends and family fight and a tragic mistake leads Romeo and Juliet to die.

> "What's in a name? That which we call a rose
> By any other name would smell as sweet"

Holy Trinity Church, location of Shakespeare's graves

Plaque on Anne's grave

William's grave, center, and Anne's grave, right,

Plaque on William's grave

Furthermore, there is no record of his education. While other playwrights came from the famous universities Oxford and Cambridge, Shakespeare is not known to have attended any university. In fact, Shakespeare even signed and spelled his name several different ways.

Does that mean he was actually uneducated? Probably not, but there is no explanation in what we know of his background for how he became so successful as a playwright. This lack of historical record and evidence is the basis for conspiracy, an opportunity for some people to imagine and construct different theories about what we don't know.

LEARN MORE

Do a deep dive on Shakespeare. What else can you discover about his life, death, hometown, and the authorship question?

Shakespeare's Birthplace Trust: https://shakespeare.org.uk

Shakespeare's Globe:
https://www.shakespearesglobe.com/discover/shakespeares-world/

Internet Shakespeare Editions
https://internetshakespeare.uvic.ca/Library/SLT/intro/index.html

Find out more about the life, plays, and mysteries of Christopher Marlowe at the Marlowe Society: https://www.marlowe-society.org/marlowe/

Read more of Shakespeare's sonnets and discover other poets at the Poetry Foundation:
https://www.poetryfoundation.org/poets/william-shakespeare

Study the plays of Shakespeare yourself at OpenSource Shakespeare:
https://www.opensourceshakespeare.org/views/plays/plays_alpha.php

Find summaries and analysis of his plays at The Royal Shakespeare Company's Learning Zone: https://www.rsc.org.uk/shakespeare-learning-zone

Find which contemporary plays are touring and make plans to see one on stage in your city: https://playbill.com/shows/touring

THE THEORIES

Shakespeare was a group project

Delia Bacon

One of the first theories that doubted the identity of Shakespeare claimed a group of writers were the real authors. An American author and literary scholar named Delia Bacon traveled to England to prove this theory, and she even tried to open Shakespeare's grave where she thought she would find papers hidden by the collaborators. Ultimately, she was unsuccessful digging anything up or finding any evidence to support her group project theory.

Delia Bacon's main argument was her belief that Shakespeare's plays were written about philosophical topics with coded information in order to influence political ideas. She was sure a man with Shakespeare's apparent background couldn't have done it. She and her supporters believed famous aristocrats, philosophers and writers of Shakespeare's time—such as Sir Francis Bacon, Sir Walter Raleigh and Edmund Spenser—collaborated on the plays as a project and left clues in the text as a kind of secret code for other philosophers to decipher.

Edmund Spencer

Delia lived in the mid-19th century at the same time as another famous English author, Charles Dickens, who was writing stories as social commentary and criticism. So, perhaps it's not surprising that a literary scholar like her would have thought Shakespeare's plays had similar purposes. But her theory is also largely based on her prejudice—her belief that someone with Shakespeare's humble, rural background could never become a good playwright.

Setting aside the unproven theory about a code, the case for Delia's group theory relies solely on the style and purpose of Shakespeare's writing and does not have any strong evidence linking the work to other men or women. Other group theories that have been suggested share the assumption that Shakespeare did not have the education and background necessary to write about the themes and topics in his plays.

Shakespeare was Edward de Vere, 17th Earl of Oxford

Several conspiracy theories about Shakespeare point to just one wealthy aristocrat like Sir Francis Bacon or Sir Walter Raleigh, but the man who is most often believed to be the "real" Shakespeare is Edward de Vere, the 17th Earl of Oxford. He was a wealthy patron of the theater and also a poet. Conspiracy theorists have noted many connections between Shakespeare and the Earl. For example, the notes in the Earl's Bible connect to biblical language in Shakespeare's plays, and Shakespeare is famous for using a poetic form, the sonnet, that Edward de Vere's uncle invented.

Edward De Vere

The conspiracy theory also hinges on the Earl's own identity as an author. Those who support the theory believe it's no coincidence that even though the Earl was an active patron of the theater and a writer, there are no plays attributed to him. Could he have been secretly writing plays under the pseudonym Shakespeare?

One argument against this theory is that the earl died in 1604 before many of Shakespeare's plays are believed to have been written. And like the group theory, the evidence that supports this conspiracy relies heavily on making guesses about coincidences and doubting the qualifications of Shakespeare's Stratford background.

Sidebar Sonnets and poetry

Shakespeare's plays are his most famous work, but he also wrote 154 sonnets and other poems. His poem "Shall I compare thee to a summer's day?" might be as famous as any of his plays. Most of Shakespeare's poetry follows a particular form called a sonnet, and "Shall I compare thee..." is also called Sonnet 18.

To write an English sonnet, a poet must follow a few rules: The poem must be 14 lines, it must follow a strict rhyme pattern that ends with a rhyming couplet, and each line should have the same rhythm and number of syllables. A sonnet's rhythm and **syllable** count are called iambic pentameter.

Read Sonnet 18, and notice how the first line rhymes with the third and the second with the fourth. The poem follows this pattern until the final two lines rhyme with each other. Do you hear the rhythm of ten syllables repeating in each line?

Sonnet 18: Shall I compare thee to a summer's day?

Shall I compare thee to a summer's day?
Thou art more lovely and more temperate:
Rough winds do shake the darling buds of May,
And summer's lease hath all too short a date;
Sometime too hot the eye of heaven shines,
And often is his gold complexion dimm'd;
And every fair from fair sometime declines,
By chance or nature's changing course untrimm'd;
But thy eternal summer shall not fade,
Nor lose possession of that fair thou ow'st;
Nor shall death brag thou wander'st in his shade,
When in eternal lines to time thou grow'st:
    So long as men can breathe or eyes can see,
    So long lives this, and this gives life to thee.

You don't have to follow the rules for sonnets in order to write a poem. There are many other famous forms, such as the *haiku* from Japanese poetry or the *ghazal* from Arabic poetry. And many poets don't follow any special form when they write. Your poem could be more than 50 lines or only two lines, and it doesn't have to rhyme at all. It might not be a sonnet, but it can still be a good poem.

Shakespeare was Christopher Marlowe

Of the many theories that have been suggested, one of the most dramatic is that Christopher Marlowe was Shakespeare. Marlowe was a well-known and successful playwright in England who wrote plays much like Shakespeare. In fact, some scholars think Shakespeare might have been influenced by Marlowe because of similarities in their work. Conspiracy theorists believe the similarities are evidence that Marlowe and Shakespeare are the same person. One of Marlowe's most famous plays is *Doctor Faustus*, about a man who makes a deal with the devil.

Possible portrait of Christopher Marlowe

Some people think Marlowe also made a deal with his own life. Marlowe was not alive when Shakespeare became popular because he was murdered in Deptford, London in 1593. At least, that is the official story. The circumstances of his death are somewhat mysterious and the official report was not made public until 1925. Marlowe had been accused of atheism, which was a serious crime at that time in England, and some scholars speculate he faked his death to avoid punishment or was assassinated by political enemies. Additionally, historians think he himself was possibly working as a spy. The house where he died is thought to have been a safehouse for government agents, and the men who were with him when he died all had

Ruins of Scadbury Manor, where Marlowe was staying when he was killed connections to Queen Elizabeth's spymaster. These men had to be experts at keeping secrets, and it is likely they knew how to fake a murder.

The final piece of evidence that supports the Marlowe conspiracy theory is that all of Shakespeare's work was published after Marlowe's death. Although they were the same age, their public careers did not overlap. Is it only a coincidence that Shakespeare's name first appeared in print just a few weeks after Marlowe's murder? Conspiracy theorists take this information as evidence Marlowe didn't really die but went into hiding and started using Shakespeare as his pseudonym. But like the other theories that have been argued, the Christopher Marlowe theory relies mostly on coincidental dates and style similarities and no actual evidence that Marlowe faked his death or wrote Shakespeare.

Where is the evidence?

Most historians and literary scholars don't believe there was any conspiracy. They believe that William Shakespeare was a real man and the real author of all the famous work, and they note that there is no strong evidence that supports any of the conspiracy theories. We do have evidence William Shakespeare was born and died in Stratford, and his name is connected to the famous plays and poetry. No conspiracies about his identity were argued until Delia Bacon's group theory over 200 years after his death. Most scholars say the information we do know is good enough to dismiss the conspiracies. They say the theories amount to nothing more than sensational guesses about coincidences and missing records.

Perhaps the dramatic stories in Shakespeare's plays like Hamlet and Macbeth inspired the conspiracy theorists to see drama in Shakespeare's own life story where there was none. Or perhaps there actually is something surprising about Shakespeare's life that we don't know because of lost records. But do you think it's possible any of the conspiracy theories are true? If so, how would you prove your case?

WHY DOES IT MATTER

Shakespeare is one of the most famous authors who has been culturally significant and influential for hundreds of years. Knowing the truth about his identity would help us better understand the origin and inspiration for many characteristics of our contemporary culture—particularly in the areas of language, arts, and entertainment.

Shakespeare's plays are often adapted and enjoyed as movies. Consider the following list. Have you seen any of these versions of his stories?

10 Things I Hate about You (1999) — A teen romantic comedy based on *The Taming of the Shrew*

'Get Over It' (2001) — *A Midsummer Night's Dream* set in a US high-school

Gnomeo & Juliet (2011) — A lighthearted animated take on *Romeo and Juliet*

Hamlet (2000) — A modern gritty version of *Hamlet* set in New York

O (2001) — A high school drama inspired by *Othello*

Romeo + Juliet (1996) — A modern take on *Romeo and Juliet* for teens that keeps the original language

She's the Man (2006) — A teen romantic comedy based on *Twelfth Night*

The King (2019) — A gritty telling of *Henry V*

The Lion King (1994) — An animated children's movie roughly based on *Hamlet*

West Side Story (1961) — A musical version of *Romeo and Juliet* that uses rival gangs instead of feuding families

FUN FACTS

Romeo and Juliet may be the most performed play of all time. Famous versions include the 1996 movie with Leonardo DiCaprio and the 1957 Broadway adaptation *West Side Story*.

When Lord Chamberlain's Men built The Globe, the actors themselves carried the wood from an old theater across the River Thames in order to build the new one.

Some actors believe *Macbeth* is a cursed play and that saying its name will bring bad luck. This superstition causes them to say "the Scottish play" or "Macb" instead of the full name.

GLOSSARY

atheism (n.) — Believing there is no god

attribute (v.) — To identify the source or cause

basis (n.) — Foundation, the original factor

conspiracy (n.) — A secret plan to do something bad

decipher (v.) — To understand or read a code

hinge on (phrasal v.) — Rely on, need for support

patron (n.) — Person who supports by giving money

prolific (adj.) — Doing something a lot and often

pseudonym (n.) — a fake name to hide identity

reconstruction (n.) — something rebuilt after being destroyed

scholar (n.) — Person who studies deeply

speculate (v.) — Guess what is possible or likely

theory (n.) — Explanation or idea that is missing evidence

safehouse (n.) — A house used to hide spies or criminals

DISCUSSION QUESTIONS

1. Which conspiracy theory do you think is most convincing? Why?
   - Do you believe Shakespeare might be a pseudonym?

2. Does it matter if Shakespeare is fake?
   - Why do you think people like to investigate conspiracies about Shakespeare?

3. Do you think it is possible Christopher Marlowe successfully faked his death?
   - How could he have accomplished it?
   - Can you imagine a situation where you would try to fake your death? Explain.

4. Why do you think Shakespeare became the most famous English author?
   - What makes his work so popular?

5. Have you ever read or written poetry?
   - What kind of poem was it?
   - What was it about?
   - Did it rhyme?
   - Did you like it?

PROJECTS

1. Describe your own theory: Write about one page to describe who Shake-speare really was. How did he (or she, or they) become so good at writing? If your theory is that Shakespeare is a pseudonym, why did the author need one?

2. Watch a movie based on one of Shakespeare's plays and write a review. Give a summary of the story and your opinion of the movie. What details were interesting to you?

3. Choose one of Shakespeare's poems for a class presentation. Explain the theme and give your opinion. Read it aloud or challenge yourself to recite it all from memory.

4. Write a sonnet: Choose a topic you like and write fourteen lines with a rhyming couplet at the end. Can you make every line iambic pentame-ter? Read some sonnet examples first to get the feeling of the rhythm. OR choose a different form like a Haiku or Ghazal and try to follow the rules. OR make up your own poetry form!

5. Research the life and death of a famous author from your home country. Create a visual presentation that shares the major events of their life and gives examples of the literature they are famous for. Are there any mys-teries about their life?

REFERENCES

Barber, Rosalind. "Shakespeare Authorship Doubt in 1593". *Critical Survey*, 21, (2009) : 83-110. Accessed August 23, 2020. http://www.jstor.org/stable/41556314

"Discover." Shakespeare's Globe. October 31, 2025. Accessed June 19, 2020. https://www.shakespearesglobe.com/discover

Kathman, David, and Terry Ross. "The Shakespeare Authorship Page."/. Accessed June 19, 2025. https://shakespeareauthorship.com

Nicholl, Charles. "Death in Deptford." May 15, 1930. Accessed June 19, 2025. https://www.marlowe-society.org/christopher-marlowe/life/death-in-deptford

Landrigan, Leslie. "Delia Bacon, Driven Crazy By William Shakespeare." New England Historical Society. February 2, 2014. Accessed June 19, 2025. https://newenglandhistoricalsociety.com/delia-bacon-driven-crazy-william-shakespeare

Lets Talk Shakespeare podcast. "How Much Was Shakespeare Worth?." Shakespeare Birthplace Trust. Accessed June 19, 2025. https://www.shakespeare.org.uk/explore-shakespeare/podcasts/lets-talk-shakespeare/how-much-was-shakespeare-worth/.

"Marlovian theory of Shakespeare authorship." Wikipedia. May 3, 2006. Accessed June 19, 2025. https://en.wikipedia.org/wiki/Marlovian_theory_of_Shakespeare_authorship

Pruitt, Sarah. "Did Shakespeare Really Write His Own Plays?." HISTORY. July 15, 2015. Accessed June 19, 2025. https://www.history.com/news/did-shakespeare-really-write-his-own-plays

"Shakespeare authorship question." Wikipedia. February 12, 2002. Accessed June 19, 2025. https://en.wikipedia.org/wiki/Shakespeare_authorship_question

"Shakespeare's Globe Theatre." Shakespeare Birthplace Trust. Accessed June 19, 2025. https://www.shakespeare.org.uk/explore-shakespeare/shakespedia/shakespeares-globe-theatre

"Shakespeare's 'Lost Years'." Shakespeare Birthplace Trust. Accessed June 19, 2025. https://www.shakespeare.org.uk/explore-shakespeare/shakespedia/william-shakespeare/shakespeares-lost-years

Shapiro, James. *Contested Will: Who wrote Shakespeare?*. Simon & Schuster, 2011.

"The Marlowe Society." The Marlowe Society Home Page. Accessed June 19, 2025. https://www.marlowe-society.org

"William Shakespeare." The Poetry Foundation. Accessed June 19, 2025. https://www.poetryfoundation.org/poets/william-shakespeare

"William Shakespeare." Wikipedia. October 14, 2001. Accessed June 19, 2025. https://en.wikipedia.org/wiki/William_Shakespeare

ISBN: 978-1-956159-64-6 (print)

For permission requests, write to the publisher at "ATTN: Permissions", at the address below:

29 Milo Dr. Branford, CT 06405 USA
info@alphabetpublishingbooks.com
www.AlphabetPublishingBooks.com

Discounts on class sets and bulk orders available upon inquiry.

Cover and Interior Design by Walton Burns

Country of Manufacture Specified on Last Page

First Printing 2025

Images

cover left Wikimedia/Unknown, PD • cover center Wikimedia/Samuel Cousins, PD • cover right Wikimedia/Unknown, PD • pg. i Wikimedia/The New Student Reference, PD • pg. ii top Wikimedia/Des Bleninsopp, CC by-SA 2.0 • pg. ii middle Wikimedia/The New Student Reference, PD • pg. ii bottom Wikimedia/Martinvlr, CC by-SA 4.0 • pg. 6 top Wikimedia/attr. to John Taylor, PD • pg. 6 middle Wikimedia/Nathaniel Curzon, PD • pg. 6 bottom Wikimedia/Grant Cherrington, CC by-SA 2.0 • pg. 7 top Wikimedia/Nigel Swales, CC by-SA 2.0 • pg. 7 bottom Walton Burns/Open Street Map, CC by-SA 4.0 • pg. 8 Yale Center for British Art/Unknown, CC 0 • pg. 9 top Wikimedia/Christine Matthews, CC by-SA 2.0 • pg. 9 bottom Wikimedia/Jack1958, CC 0 1.0 • pg. 10 Wikimedia/Unknown, PD • pg. 11 Shakespearesglobe.com/William Shakespeare, PD • pg. 12 top Wikimedia/Len Williams, CC by-SA 2.0 • pg. 12 top middle Wikimedia/Tom Reedy, CC by-SA 3.0 • pg. 12 bottom middle Wikimedia/Bin im Garten, CC by-SA 3.0 • pg. 12 bottom Wikimedia/Lewis Clarke, CC by-SA 2.0 • pg. 14 top Wikimedia/Theodore Bacon, PD • pg. 14 bottom Wikimedia/Unknown, PD • pg. 15 Wikimedia/Unknown, PD • pg. 18 top Wikimedia/Unknown, PD • pg. 18 bottom Wikimedia/Ethan Doyle White, CC by-SA 4.0 • pg. 21 all DepositPhotos/Steiner14, licensed

www.ingramcontent.com/pod-product-compliance
Lightning Source LLC
Chambersburg PA
CBHW041448120626
46547CB00002B/389